1 MONTH OF
FREE
READING

at
www.ForgottenBooks.com

By purchasing this book you are eligible for one month membership to ForgottenBooks.com, giving you unlimited access to our entire collection of over 1,000,000 titles via our web site and mobile apps.

To claim your free month visit:
www.forgottenbooks.com/free1118628

ISBN 978-0-331-40080-9
PIBN 11118628

FOREIGN CROPS AND MARKETS

ISSUED WEEKLY BY THE BUREAU OF AGRICULTURAL ECONOMICS.
UNITED STATES DEPARTMENT OF AGRICULTURE, WASHINGTON, D.C.

VOLUME 17   DECEMBER 24, 1928   NO. 26

WHEAT AND BARLEY ACREAGE IN JAPAN

The wheat area harvested in Japan in 1928 is estimated at 1,198,000 acres according to a cable to the Foreign Service of the Bureau of Agricultural Economics from the International Institute of Agriculture. This represents an increase over the area harvested in any year since 1922. The area harvested in 1927 was estimated at 1,161,000 acres and in 1926 at 1,146,000 acres. A previous report received from the Institute has placed the 1928 wheat production at 31,196,000 bushels compared with 31,018,000 bushels in 1927. The barley area harvested in 1928 is estimated at 2,240,000 acres, which is a decrease of 4.4 per cent from the 2,343,000 acres harvested in 1927. In 1926, the area harvested amounted to 2,431,000 acres, and in 1925 to 2,466,000 acres. The 1928 production, as estimated by the Institute is 83,505,000 bushels compared with 82,485,000 bushels in 1927.

- - - - - - - - - - - -

CURRENT MARKET CONDITIONS

Continued heavy purchases of raw cotton in Japan is indicated by the increased activity of the spinning and weaving mills during November. The amount of yarn produced by the spinning mills and consumed by weavers shows increases over November of last year, according to a cable from Consul Dickover, at Kobe. Buying of American cotton for future delivery in Osaka, however, was reported slow late in November due to the large amounts already contracted for. Production of yarn in November for all Japan reached 217,000 bales of 400 pounds, compared with 211,000 bales in October and 208,000 in November 1927. Consumption of yarn by weaving mills was 68,200 bales in November, 63,700 in October and 60,937 for November of last year. Imports of American cotton totaled 92,000 bales in November 1928, and 81,000 for the same month a year ago. Stocks of cotton of all kinds in bonded warehouses at the end of November were 318,000 bales against 251,000 bales at the end of October and 366,000 on November 30, 1927.

The Copenhagen butter quotation as of December 20 was equivalent to 43 cents as against 49.5 cents on 92 score butter in New York. Those figures were about 1 cent lower than on the preceding Thursday, but the current London quotations on all descriptions were fully as high as a week earlier. The margin in favor of New York, therefore, continues to date at little more than half the import duty. Colonial supplies coming forward to the British markets are now heavy but the markets remained firm throughout the pre-Christmas season, as was generally anticipated. For detailed comparative statement of prices as cabled by American Agricultural Commissioners in

CROP AND MARKET PROSPECTS

- - - - - - - - - -

BREAD GRAINS

Wheat production in 1928

The 1928 wheat production in 43 countries has been reported at
3,596,250,000 bushels against 3,427,836,000   in 1927, or an increase of 4.6 per cent. The table on page 972 shows the revisions made
in accordance with the November monthly report of the International
Institute of Agriculture. See Foreign Service release, F.S./WH-30, December 22, 1928 for additional material on world wheat situation.

Foreign growing conditions

Europe

The weather in Russia during the week ended December 20 was cold,
with heavy snow in the southern section and a general snow cover in other
sections, according to cabled advices from Agricultural Commissioner
Steere at Berlin. In other parts of Europe the weather was also cold
with snow practically everywhere except in the Mediterranean countries.

Southern Hemisphere

Harvesting in Australia is nearing completion with mostly satis-
factory results, according to reports to the United States Weather Bureau.
In Argentina more favorable harvesting weather prevailed during the week
ended December 17. After the heavy rains of the past two weeks, only 0.2
inch of rain was reported in the northern wheat districts and 0.1 inch in
the southern districts.

Movement to market

United States

Exports of wheat from the United States from July 1 through Decembe
15 have amounted to 95,193,000 bushels against 152,300,000 bushels during
the same period last year. Exports during the week ended December 15 were
2,624,000 bushels against 4,847,000 bushels the previous week.

Canada

Stocks of wheat in the Western Grain Division of Canada on December
14 were 127,951,000 bushels against 79,338,000 bushels a year ago. Total
receipts at Fort William, Port Arthur, Vancouver, and Prince Rupert from
July 1 to December 14 were 262,389,000 bushels against 178,540,000 bushels

CROP AND MARKET PROSPECTS, CONT'D

- - - - - - - - - - -

during the same period last year. Shipments since July 1 have amounted to 255,642,000 bushels against 179,122,000 bushels last year.

Russia

Procurements of Russian state and cooperative grain collecting agencies during the first ten days of December amounted to 351,000 short tons compared with 258,000 short tons for a similar period last year, according to Mr. Steere at Berlin. Difficulties, however, were experienced recently with bread supply in Moscow and other urban centers, but the Soviet Government is claiming that there is no cause for anxiety although increasing efforts in procuring operations are considered necessary. The approaching spring sowing campaign in Russia is considered very important and the government is pressing for an 8 per cent increase in acreage. Resistance, however, is met with from the rich peasants, so-called "Kulaki", who are contemplating reduction of acreage. Another unfavorable factor is the probable shortage of seed in some parts of the country.

European grain markets

European wheat and flour markets continued to remain quiet during the week ended December 18, but slight improvement was noticeable in the Western European markets, according to Mr. Steere at Berlin. The United States acreage report is finding influential acceptance as marking a turning point in the wheat market. Numerous indications point to the fact that Europe bought lightly for future requirements and reports from Rumania indicate holdings for spring shipment. The price of wheat in Hamburg remained at $1.36 per bushel on December 19, or the same as reported last week, being 11 cents below the price on December 21, 1927. The price of rye at Berlin continued at $1.22 per bushel, or 21 cents below the price on December 21, 1927.

United States wheat prices

Cash wheat prices declined quite noticeably during the week ended December 14. All classes of wheat contributed to a decline of two cents in the weighted average price of all classes and grades of wheat at the six principal markets to 107 cents per bushel as compared with 129 cents last year. This is the lowest point reached since the last week in October. No. 2 hard winter at Kansas City and No. 2 soft red winter at St. Louis each dropped two cents to 111 and 141 cents respectively, as compared with 131 and 146 cents respectively a year ago. As the figures indicate, there was a spread of only 15 cents last year between these two

CROP AND MARKET PROSPECTS, CONT'D

- - - - - - - - - - -

grades of wheat at the two markets, while this year there is a spread of
30 cents. No. 1 dark northern spring at Minneapolis declined three cents
to 121 cents as compared with 137 a year ago, and No. 2 amber durum at
Minneapolis declined 10 cents to 107 cents as compared with 132 a year ago.
Western white wheat at Seattle did not participate in the decline of other
classes, but advanced slightly instead, the price for the week being 117
cents as indicated by the average of daily cash quotations, compared with
116 cents the week previous and 126 cents a year ago. Cash prices have
made no material improvement since December 14. The spread between the
cash closing prices at Winnipeg and Minneapolis narrowed two cents during
the week and was four cents in favor of Minneapolis for the week ended
December 14 as compared with a spread of four cents a year ago.

WHEAT: Weighted average cash prices at stated markets

Week ended	All classes and grades six markets		No. 2 Hard Winter Kansas City		No. 1 Dk.N.Spring Minneapolis		No. 2 Amber durum Minneapolis		No. 2 Red Winter St. Louis	
	1927	1928	1927	1928	1927	1928	1927	1928	1927	1928
	Cents	Cents	Cents	Cents	Cents	Cents	Cents	Cents	Cents	Cents
Nov. 16 ...	127	109	131	113	133	123	130	110	142	146
23 ...	127	110	134	114	134	125	128	118	142	145
30 ...	126	109	132	114	134	125	127	116	140	145
Dec. 7 ...	128	109	134	113	137	124	132	117	147	143
14 ...	129	107	131	111	137	121	132	107	146	141
21 ...	128	,	132		138		133		142	
28 ...	128		129		138		135		143	
	1928	1929	1928	1929	1928	1929	1928	1929	1928	1929
Jan. 4 ...	132		136		142		138		147	
11 ...	130		132		139		132		149	

        Trading in wheat futures was somewhat slow and dull during the week
following December 13 and the trend of closing prices was downward until
December 19 when May futures at Chicago advanced approximately one cent,
apparently on the strength of the lower official estimates of the acreage
and condition of winter wheat. Prices declined again on the day following,
however. On December 20, the closing prices of May futures as compared
with the week before were one cent lower at Chicago, Kansas City, and Minneapolis in the United States, and at Winnipeg. The Liverpool price was
unchanged at 134 cents as compared with 149 cents a year ago. The Chicago
close was 121 cents as compared with 170 last year, while the Winnipeg
close was 123 cents, or 12 cents less than a year ago. February futures
at Buenos Aires closed at 114 cents on December 19, or 4 cents higher than
a week before and 13 cents less than last year.

CROP AND MARKET PROSPECTS, CONT'D

- - - - - - - - - - - -

WHEAT: Closing prices of December and May futures

ate	Chicago		Kansas City		Minneapolis		Winnipeg		Liverpool		Buenos Aires a/	
	1927	1928	1927	1928	1927	1928	1927	1928	1927	1928	1927	1928
					December futures							
Nov.15	128	116	123	110	124	111	132	120	152	135	b/129	b/115
22	132	117	123	110	124	112	132	119	152	135	b/131	b/116
29	129	115	123	109	125	111	133	117	151	134	b/127	b/113
					May futures							
Dec. 6	134	122	127	115	130	116	137	123	150	133	b/127	b/112
13	130	122	124	115	126	116	135	124	149	134	b/127	b/110
20	130	121	124	114	126	115	135	123	149	134	b/127	b/114
27	130		124		126		136		149		b/126	
	1928	1929	1928	1929	1928	1929	1928	1929	1928	1929	1928	1929
Jan. 3	131		125		128		137		152		b/129	
10	131		125		128		136		149		b/126	

a/ Prices are as of day previous to date of other market prices.   b/ February
futures.

Rye production

     The 1928 rye production in 24 countries is now reported at 889,681,000
bushels against 842,840,000 bushels in 1927, or an increase of 5.6 per cent.
See table, page 972.

FEED GRAINS

     The total production of the three feed grains, barley, oats and corn,
in the European countries so far reported in 1928 amounts to 52,267,000 short
tons, according to the latest estimates, compared with 53,131,000 short tons
in 1927, 59,612,000 short tons in 1926, 56,279,000 short tons in 1925, and a
pre-war average in 1909-1913 of 57,617,000 short tons.

Barley

     Total production of barley in the 38 countries so far reported in 1928,
which last year raised about 80 per cent of the world crop exclusive of Russia
and China, now stands at 1,395,370,000 bushels, an increase of more than 16
per cent over the 1,202,314,000 bushels produced in the same countries last
year. The first estimate of the 1928 barley crop of Scotland is 4,433,000
bushels, which is 1 per cent larger than the 1927 harvest, but which is, with
that exception, the smallest crop on record. This new estimate for Scotland

CROP AND MARKET PROSPECTS, CONT'D

- - - - - -- - - - - - - -

and slight increases in the earlier estimates of barley production in Es-
tonia and Luxemburg raise the European total for the 24 countries reported
to 667,663,000 bushels, or 7.8 per cent above that of the same countries
in 1927.

The Algerian production has been increased by nearly 1,400,000
bushels from the earlier estimate to 38,122,000 bushels, which raises the
total for the 6 North African countries reported to 105,003,000 bushels,
a figure more than 22 per cent above that of 1927. For barley production
table, see page 973. The barley area harvested in Japan in 1928 is estimated at 2,240,000 acres, which is a decrease of 4.4 per cent from the
2,343,000 acres harvested in 1927. In 1926, the area harvested amounted
to 2,431,000 acres, and in 1925 to 2,466,000 acres. The 1928 production
is 83,505,000 bushels compared with 82,485,000 bushels in 1927.

Total barley exports from the United States, Canada, Argentina,
and the Danubian countries from July 1 to the latest dates available
amount to 77,827,000 bushels against 62,457,000 bushels for the same periods last year. The United States export of 588,000 bushels for the week
ended December 15 was one of the smallest, since the first week in August.
There has not been much change in United States barley prices during the
past week. No. 2 barley at Minneapolis averaged 62 cents per bushel for the
week ended December 14, which was 1 cent below the price for the preceding
week and 20 cents below the price for the corresponding week last year.

Exports of barley from Canada from July to November are much larger
than for the same five-month period last year, amounting to 21,636,000
bushels compared with 12,016,000 bushels. Stocks in store in the Western
Grain Inspection Division of Canada on December 14 stood at 11,524,000
bushels against 6,202,000 bushels on the same date in 1927, and 7,843,000
bushels in 1926.

Oats

The total oats production in 31 countries, which last year raised
nearly 91 per cent of the world crop, exclusive of Russia and China,
stands at 3,576,898,000 bushels, an increase of 9.5 per cent over the
3,267,458,000 bushels raised in 1927. The first estimate of the 1928 oats
crop in Scotland is 46,771,000 bushels. This is an increase of nearly 8
per cent over the 1927 crop, but below the production from 1924 to 1926.
This estimate for Scotland with an increase of nearly 600,000 bushels in
the earlier figure for the crop of Luxemburg raises the European total for
the 23 countries reported to 1,664,332,000 bushels, or 2.4 per cent above
the production for the same countries in 1927. For table showing oats
production, see page 974.

CROP AND MARKET PROSPECTS, CONT'D

- - - - - - - - - - - -

Total exports of oats from the United States, Canada, Argentina, and the Danubian countries as far as reported from July 1 to the latest dates available now amount to 21,390,000 bushels as compared with 17,689,000 bushels for the same periods last year. The export of 349,000 buehsle from the United States for the week ended December 15 was the largest since the first week in November. Oats exports from Canada for the five-month period July - November were several times as large as for the same period last year. For 10,914,000 bushels compared with 2,892,000 bushels last year.

United States oats prices remain at about the same level as for the past few weeks. No. 3 white oats at Chicago averaged 47 cents per bushel during the week ended December 14. This was the same price as for the preceding week, but 8 cents below the price for the corresponding week last year. Oats prices in Germany were reported to be somewhat lower early in December. Stocks of oats in store in the Western Grain Inspection Division of Canada on December 14 stood at 11,303,000 bushels compared with 8,517,000 bushels on the same date in 1927, and 8,261,000 bushels in 1926. For detailed figures on oats trade, see page 976.

Corn

The 1928 production of corn in 17 countries, which last year raised 90 per cent of the Northern Hemisphere crop exclusive of Russia, now totals 3,266,896,000 bushels, or 0.5 per cent below the production of 3,284,140,000 bushels in the same countries last year. During the past week there has been a slight increase in the earlier estimate for Spain, but this has been more than offset by a decrease of 1,200,000 bushels in the latest estimate for Hungary, which changes leave the total production for the 9 European countries reported only 343,343,000 bushels compared with 437,960,000 bushels last year.

In Asia the earlier estimate for Manchuria has been decreased considerably, while the figures for the Lebanon Republic and Alaouite are below those of last year. The total for the Asiatic countries reported is, therefore, 2.4 per cent below that for the same countries in 1927. The estimated European, Northern Hemisphere, and world totals for corn production in 1925, 1926, and 1927 have been changed a little, owing to numerous estimates and revisions which have been recently received for the minor corn producing countries for those years. A detailed table for corn production is found on page 975. Reports received from most of the departments of Greece, which last year supplied about 92 per cent of the total, show a production of about 4,212,000 bushels against 4,698,000 bushels last year. Since the report is not complete for the country, it is not included in the corn production table.

CROP AND MARKET PROSPECTS, CONT'D

- - - - - - - - - - -

The area sown to winter corn in Egypt in 1928 is 13,000 acres compared with 19,000 acres in 1927, from which 752,000 bushels were harvested.

Exports of corn from the United States, the Danubian countries, Argentina, and the Union of South Africa so far as reported since November 1 total 37,501,000 bushels compared with 44,537,000 bushels for the same periods last year. The United States export of 1,443,000 bushels during the week ended December 15 and the export of 1,699,000 bushels during the preceding week were the largest weekly exports for several seasons. The Argentine shipment of 4,249,000 bushels during the week of December 15, while 1,500,000 bushels below that of the preceding week, is nearly up to the weekly average during the past two months.

There has been no marked change in United States corn prices recently, while Argentine prices for the week December 12 - 19 have generally been gradually increasing, the last quotation received being 96-1/2 cents on December 19. Argentine corn prices still remain more than 10 cents per bushel above United States prices, while last year at the same time United States prices were slightly higher. Reports from abroad indicate that Argentina is giving slightly lower quotations for corn from the harvest of the new crop, but heavy deliveries cannot be expected before next July and August.

During the first few days of December the Danish interest in Argentine corn was slightly weaker and the quotations declined slightly, according to the Danish publication, "Grain and Feedstuffs", of December 5. This reduction in prices in Argentina refers especially to the new crop La Plata corn for May and June shipments, but on account of the long journey the corn cannot be delivered in Europe before during July and August. There are shipments of new corn from Argentina in April, but for such shipments quotations were higher, owing to the limited quantities which can be shipped as early as in April. The firm North American corn prices have led Danish buyers to expect that corn will continue to be expensive until the new Argentine crop appears, which, as stated above, cannot occur for several month It is held as being fortunate for Denmark's large hog industry that the grai harvest in that country has been large, and that the cheaper feed wheat and probably also tapioca meal can be substituted for corn. The quotations for feed barley in Denmark had declined by December 5, and cost considerably less than corn so increases in consumption of foreign barley were expected, especially later on when the supply of Danish barley begins to dwindle.

C R O P   A N D   M A R K E T   P R O S P E C T S,   C O N T'D

- - - - - - - - - - - -

RICE

The second estimate of acreage under rice in India for 1928 is 79,258,000 acres, or 6 per cent above the second estimate last year, and 2 per cent above the final figure for last year, according to a cable to the Bureau of Agricultural Economics from the International Institute of Agriculture under date of December 20. The second estimate this year, while 6 per cent above last, is also 2 per cent above the average for the five years 1922 to 1926. See table, page 975.

- - - - - - - - - - - -

COTTON

The first estimate of the cotton crop in India is 5,013,000 bales of 478 pounds, or 109 per cent of the December estimate of last year, according to a cablegram received by the Foreign Service of the Bureau of Agricultural Economics from the Indian Department of Statistics of Calcutta. The final estimate for the 1927-28 season was 4,913,000 bales and for 1926-27, 4,205,000. Acreage planted to cotton in India this season is now placed at 24,992,000, or 108 per cent of the December estimate last year. The final acreage estimate for last season was 24,722,000 acres.

- - - - - - - - - - - -

SUGAR

The import duty on sugar in Germany has been raised from $32 to $54 per short ton, according to a cablegram from Agricultural Commissioner L. V. Steere at Berlin. The new rate became effective on December 18 and will remain in effect for three years.

- - - - - - - - - - - -

SUGAR BEETS

Revised estimates received to date bring the total acreage devoted to sugar beets in Europe, United States and Canada up to 7,353,000 acres as compared with the previously published estimate of 7,318,000 acres. (See "Foreign Crops and Markets", November 26, 1928, page 840.) Increases over early estimates occur in the United States, Denmark, Germany, and Austria.

Production statistics show a slight decline from the October 26 estimate, which is mostly accounted for by a reduction of 2,322,000 short

CROP AND MARKET PROSPECTS, CONT'D

- - - - - - - - - - -

tons in the Russian Crop. The revised estimate for Russia indicates a
crop about 4 per cent below that of 1927, which is contrary to early ex-
pectations in view of the fact that acreage statistics showed an increase of 19.5 per cent over last year. The yield in 1927, however, was
unusually high. Acreage and production of sugar beets are summarized on
page 978.

- - - - - - - - - - - -

FRUIT, VEGETABLES AND NUTS

- - - - - - - - - - - -

THE BRITISH APPLE MARKET: There was a good demand for American
apples on the Liverpool auction on Wednesday, December 19, according to
a cable received in the Foreign Service of the Bureau of Agricultural
Economics from Mr. Edwin Smith, the Department's Fruit Specialist in
Europe. Barreled stock was only in light supply, but boxed supplies
were liberal. The condition of the fruit, with a few exceptions, was
good. Prices on most varieties were higher than last week. There was
an active demand for U. S. No. 1, 2-1/2 inch New York Rhode Island Green-
ings. Virginia Yorks also met with an active demand. There was a good
demand for the light supplies of Baldwins available. Oregon Spitzen-
bergs were in liberal supply and met with only a moderate demand, due
probably to the fact that much of the fruit was in variable condition.
Oregon Newtowns were in moderate supply and met with a good demand.
Oregon Delicious were in moderate supply but met with only a slow demand.
The light supplies of Oregon Hood River Jonathans available met with an
active demand.

The Spanish orange market in Great Britain is showing strength.
The fruit is arriving clean and attractive and is in good condition.
Supplies this year are liberal, being only 8 per cent below last year's
large quantities. New crop South African plums and peaches are beginning to arrive and the first pears for the season from that country will
be available about February 1. The South African fruit crops this year
are reported about 30 per cent lighter than last year. The 1929 apple
crop in Australia is reported to be considerably below that for 1928.
The crop in Victoria and New South Wales is said to be negligible. The
Tasmanian crop is reported light, but Western Australia is expected to
have a normal yield. The New Zealand crop is reported as normal. Book-
ings are already being made for Australian and New Zealand apples at
high prices. The April market outlook for American apples is favorable,
states Mr. Smith. See Foreign Service release, F.S./A-209, December 21,
1928.

FRUIT, VEGETABLES AND NUTS, CONT'D

- - - - - - - - - -

THE HAMBURG APPLE MARKET: Prices paid for American apples at the Hamburg auction on Thursday, December 20, indicate that the market is showing strength, according to a cable received in the Foreign Service of the Bureau of Agricultural Economics from Mr. Edwin Smith, the Department's Fruit Specialist in Europe. A total of 19,300 barrels and 52,700 boxes were offered as compared with 20,000 and 105,500 boxes last week. Virginia Yorks brought $5.24 to $6.91 as compared with $4.29 to $6.43 last week for U. S. No. 1, 2-1/4 inch stock. Prices on boxed stock were practically the same as those prevailing last week. See Foreign Service release, F.S./A-210, December 21, 1928.

MEXICAN VEGETABLE PROSPECTS: All indications point to a favorable season in the Mexican West Coast vegetable industry this year, according to a report received in the Foreign Service of the Bureau of Agricultural Economics from Consul Henry C. A. Damm at Nogales, Sonora, Mexico. No insect pests have been reported and no areas have suffered from heavy rains, winds or frosts. Southern Sonora did not get its summer rains as early as it should in order to place the soil in proper condition for planting, but the only result will be a slight delay in the crop. As far as can be learned at present, the total vegetable acreage on the West Coast this season will be about the same as last year, but no estimates of the probable number of cars to be shipped have been made as yet. See Foreign Service release, F.S./V-35, December 17, 1928.

SPANISH GRANO ONION SHIPMENTS: Shipments of grano onions from Spain to the United States from December 6 to December 19, 1928, amounted to 6,502 half-cases and 10,162 crates, according to a cable received in the Foreign Service of the Bureau of Agricultural Economics from Consul Clement S. Edwards at Valencia. With these shipments the total movement of grano onions to the American market from the beginning of the season late in July to December 19 amounted to 2,927 cases, 310,113 half-cases, and 669,660 crates, or approximately 882,000 bushels, as compared with 556,000 bushels during the corresponding period last year.

BREAD GRAINS: Production, average 1909-1913, annual 1925-1928

Crop and countries reported in 1928 a/	Average 1909-1913	1925	1926	1927	1928	Per cent 1928 is of 1927
WHEAT	1,000 bushels	1,000 bushels	1,000 bushels	1,000 bushels	1,000 bushels	Per cent
United States	690,108	676,429	831,040	878,374	902,749	102.8
Canada	197,119	395,475	407,136	440,025	500,613	113.8
North America (3)	898,708	1,081,117	1,248,509	1,330,289	1,414,694	106.3
Europe, 22 count. prev. reported	1,312,987	1,353,061	1,167,329	1,223,506	1,328,367	108.6
Scotland	2,273	2,016	2,091	2,427	2,256	93.0
Luxemburg, revised	615	553	622	702	799	113.8
Greece, revised	b/ 16,273	11,222	12,403	12,970	15,676	120.9
Total Europe (25)	1,332,148	1,366,852	1,182,445	1,239,605	1,347,098	108.7
Africa (6)	93,171	105,166	90,313	105,763	105,733	100.0
Asia (6)	387,827	382,847	379,294	389,636	337,452	86.6
Total above count. (40)	2,711,854	2,935,932	2,900,561	3,065,293	3,204,977	104.6
Southern Hemis., 2 count. prev. rept'd	153,093	200,351	228,870	245,806	237,273	96.5
Australia, revised	90,497	114,504	160,762	116,737	154,000	131.9
Total Southern. Hemis. (3)	243,590	314,855	389,632	362,543	391,273	107.9
Total above count. (43)	2,955,444	3,250,787	3,290,193	3,427,836	3,596,250	104.9
Est. N. Hemis. total ex. Russia & China...	2,759,000	3,067,000	2,979,000	3,137,000		
Est. world total ex. Russia and China	3,041,000	3,435,000	3,420,000	3,565,000	3,730,000	104.6
RYE						
United States	36,093	46,456	40,795	58,164	41,766	71.8
Canada	2,094	9,158	12,179	14,951	14,626	97.8
Europe, 19 count. prev. reported	910,868	886,556	696,122	758,543	819,328	108.0
Luxemburg, revised	651	360	353	354	354	100.0
Greece, revised	1,129	1,566	1,412	1,505	2,124	141.1
Rumania, revised	20,644	7,997	11,243	9,323	11,483	123.3
Total Europe (22)	933,292	896,479	709,129	769,725	833,289	108.3
Total above count. (24)	971,479	952,093	762,103	842,840	889,681	105.6
Est. N. Hemis. total ex. Russia and China	1,023,000	1,000,000	807,000	878,000		
Est. world total ex. Russia and China	1,025,000	1,007,000	812,000	887,000		

a/ Figures in parenthesis indicate the number of countries included.
b/ One year only.

FEED GRAINS:　Production, average 1909-1913, annual 1925-1928

Crop and countries reported in 1928 a/	Average 1909-1913	1925	1926	1927	1928	Per cent 1928 is of 1927
BARLEY	1,000 bushels	1,000 bushels	1,000 bushels	1,000 bushels	1,000 bushels	Per cent
alifornia, revised	37,690	32,550	32,400	27,335	31,842	116.5
nited States, other than California, revised ...	147,122	181,313	152,505	238,547	325,026	136.3
anada	45,275	87,118	99,987	96,938	134,452	138.7
North America (2)	230,087	300,981	284,892	362,820	491,320	135.4
rope, 21 count. prev. rept'd and unchanged .	630,539	611,936	614,681	610,574	658,832	107.9
cotland	7,173	6,347	5,087	4,387	4,433	101.0
uxemburg, revised	82	175	184	178	198	111.2
stonia, revised	6,201	5,239	6,038	4,335	4,200	96.9
Total Europe (24)	643,995	623,747	625,990	619,574	667,663	107.8
Est. European total ex. Russia	702,000	689,000	690,000	680,000		
frica, 5 count. prev. rept'd and unchanged ..	63,293	72,001	46,492	51,428	66,881	130.0
lgeria, revised	45,974	35,839	23,000	34,555	38,122	110.3
Total Africa (6)	109,267	107,840	69,492	85,983	105,003	122.1
sia (5)	153,027	138,273	136,970	133,123	130,469	98.0
Total N. Hemis. (37) ..	1,116,376	1,170,841	1,117,344	1,201,500	1,394,455	116.1
nion of South Africa ...	1,274	1,111	1,075	814	915	112.4
Total above count.(38)	1,117,650	1,171,952	1,118,419	1,202,314	1,395,370	116.1
Est. N. Hemis. total ex. Russia & China ...	1,408,000	1,456,000	1,406,000	1,477,000		
Est. world total ex. Russia and China	1,425,000	1,503,000	1,453,000	1,509,000		

/ Figures in parenthesis indicate the number of countries included.

Crop and countries reported in 1928 a/	Average 1909-1913	1925	1926	1927	1928	Per cen 192 is 192
OATS	1,000 bushels	1,000 bushels	1,000 bushels	1,000 bushels	1,000 bushels	Per cen
United States	1,143,407	1,487,550	1,246,848	1,182,594	1,449,531	122
Canada	351,690	402,296	383,416	439,713	437,505	99
North America (2) ...	1,495,097	1,889,846	1,630,264	1,622,307	1,887,036	116
Europe, 21 count. prev. rept'd and unchanged ..	1,651,874	1,511,067	1,633,231	1,578,711	1,614,430	102
Scotland	44,507	50,120	52,500	43,400	46,771	107
Luxemburg, revised	3,382	2,545	3,249	2,763	3,131	113
Total Europe (23)	1,699,763	1,563,732	1,688,980	1,624,874	1,664,332	102
Est. European total ex. Russia	1,931,000	1,792,000	1,921,000	1,843,000		
Africa (3)	17,631	19,509	11,455	13,965	18,315	131
Asia (2)	(50)	92	224	231	179	77
Total N. Hemis. (30) .	3,212,541	3,473,179	3,330,923	3,261,377	3,569,862	109
Union of South Africa ..	9,661	5,485	6,119	6,081	7,036	115
Total above count.(31)	3,222,202	3,478,664	3,337,042	3,267,458	3,576,898	109
Est. N. Hemis. total ex. Russia & China ..	3,474,000	3,729,000	3,592,000	3,503,000		
Est. world total ex. Russia and China	3,581,000	3,848,000	3,696,000	3,602,000		

a/ Figures in parenthesis indicate the number of countries included.

- - - - - - - - - - - -

POTATOES: Production, average 1909-1913, annual 1925-1928

Countries reported in 1928 a/	Average 1909-1913	1925	1926	1927	1928	Per cent 1928 is o 1927
	1,000 bushels	1,000 bushels	1,000 bushels	1,000 bushels	1,000 bushels	Per cent
United States	357,699	323,465	354,328	402,741	462,943	114
Canada	77,843	67,028	78,228	77,430	90,975	117
Europe, 14 count. prev. reported	2,936,885	3,372,033	2,706,428	3,357,492	3,126,687	93
England and Wales,revised	99,893	119,989	103,152	114,053	124,432	109
Scotland	34,674	37,147	33,563	29,829	38,528	129
Spain, revised	112,997	102,700	116,292	132,645	104,718	78
Austria, revised	53,373	76,001	47,695	97,973	74,864	76
Hungary, revised	71,118	84,859	68,879	73,667	47,280	64
Lithuania, revised	40,865	58,091	61,170	46,443	34,109	73
Total Europe, (20) ...	3,349,805	3,850,820	3,137,169	3,852,102	3,550,618	92
Tunis	(150)	162	154	103	165	160
Total above count.(23)	3,785,497	4,241,475	3,569,879	4,332,376	4,104,701	94

a/ Figures in parenthesis indicate the number of countries included.

FEED GRAINS: Production, average 1909-1913, annual 1925 - 1928

Crop and countries reported in 1928 a/	Average 1909-1913	1925	1926	1927	1928	Per cent 1928 is of 1927
CORN	1,000 bushels	1,000 bushels	1,000 bushels	1,000 bushels	1,000 bushels	Per cent
ted States	2,712,364	2,916,961	2,692,217	2,763,093	2,839,959	102.8
ada	17,297	10,564	7,813	4,262	4,692	110.1
orth America (2)	2,729,661	2,927,525	2,700,030	2,767,355	2,844,651	102.8
ope, 7 countries prev. ept'd and unchanged ..	447,100	465,573	533,548	343,509	276,142	80.4
in, revised	26,548	24,210	17,186	26,104	23,877	91.5
gary, revised	60,813	87,971	76,543	68,347	43,324	63.4
otal Europe (9)	534,461	581,754	627,282	437,960	343,343	78.4
ct. European total ex. Russia	581,000	626,000	665,000	479,000		
ica (3)	4,326	4,362	4,719	5,127	6,995	136.4
anon Republic,revised	(900)	433	472	512	433	84.6
ouite	(115)	(118)	276	354	236	66.7
churia, revised	(27,000)	43,206	72,144	72,832	71,238	97.8
otal Asia (3)	(28,015)	43,257	72,892	73,698	71,907	97.6
otal N. Hemis. (17) ..	3,296,463	3,557,398	3,406,075	3,284,140	3,266,896	99.5
st. N. Hemis. total ex. Russia	3,681,000	3,907,000	3,777,000	3,647,000		
st. world total ex. Russia	4,126,000	4,530,000	4,445,000	4,311,000		

Figures in parenthesis indicate the number of countries included.

RICE: Second and final estimates of acreage in India, 1922 to 1928

Year	Second estimate	Final estimate
	1,000 acres	1,000 acres
1922	78,455	82,401
1923	75,455	78,932
1924	77,763	81,328
1925	78,149	82,378
1926	77,128	79,718
1927	74,857	77,790
1928	79,256	

Crop and countries reported in 1928 a/	Average 1909-1913	1925	1926	1927	1928	P c l i l
OATS	1,000 bushels	1,000 bushels	1,000 bushels	1,000 bushels	1,000 bushels	P c
United States	1,143,407	1,487,550	1,246,848	1,182,594	1,449,531	1
Canada	351,690	402,296	383,416	439,713	437,505	
North America (2) ...	1,495,097	1,889,846	1,630,264	1,622,307	1,887,036	1
Europe, 21 count. prev. rept'd and unchanged ..	1,651,874	1,511,067	1,633,231	1,578,711	1,614,430	1
Scotland	44,507	50,120	52,500	43,400	46,771	1
Luxemburg, revised	3,382	2,545	3,249	2,763	3,131	1
Total Europe (23)	1,699,763	1,563,732	1,688,980	1,624,874	1,664,332	1
Est. European total ex. Russia	1,931,000	1,792,000	1,921,000	1,843,000		
Africa (3)	17,631	19,509	11,455	13,965	18,315	1
Asia (2)	(50)	92	224	231	179	
Total N. Hemis. (30) .	3,212,541	3,473,179	3,330,923	3,261,377	3,569,862	1
Union of South Africa ..	9,661	5,485	6,119	6,081	7,036	1
Total above count.(31)	3,222,202	3,478,664	3,337,042	3,267,458	3,576,898	1
Est. N. Hemis. total ex. Russia & China ..	3,474,000	3,729,000	3,592,000	3,509,000		
Est. world total ex. Russia and China	3,581,000	3,848,000	3,696,000	3,602,000		

a/ Figures in parenthesis indicate the number of countries included.

- - - - - - - - - - - -

POTATOES: Production, average 1909-1913, annual 1925-1928

Countries reported in 1928 a/	Average 1909-1913	1925	1926	1927	1928	Pe a 1 i 1
	1,000 bushels	1,000 bushels	1,000 bushels	1,000 bushels	1,000 bushels	P c
United States	357,699	323,465	354,328	402,741	462,943	
Canada	77,843	67,028	78,228	77,430	90,975	
Europe, 14 count. prev. reported	2,936,885	3,372,033	2,706,428	3,357,492	3,126,687	
England and Wales, revised	99,893	119,989	103,152	114,053	124,432	
Scotland	34,674	37,147	33,563	29,829	38,528	
Spain, revised	112,997	102,700	116,292	132,645	104,718	
Austria, revised	53,373	76,001	47,695	97,973	74,864	
Hungary, revised	71,118	84,859	68,879	73,667	47,280	
Lithuania, revised	40,865	58,091	61,170	46,443	34,109	
Total Europe, (20) ...	3,349,805	3,850,820	3,137,169	3,852,102	3,550,618	
Tunis	(150)	162	154	103	165	
Total above count.(23)	3,785,497	4,241,475	3,569,879	4,332,376	4,104,701	

Figures in parenthesis indicate the number of countries included.

FEED GRAINS: Production, average 1909-1913, annual 1925 - 1928

Crop and countries reported in 1928 a/	Average 1909-1913	1925	1926	1927	1928	Per cent 1928 is of 1927
CORN	1,000 bushels	1,000 bushels	1,000 bushels	1,000 bushels	1,000 bushels	Per cent
..d States	2,712,364	2,916,961	2,692,217	2,763,093	2,839,959	102.8
..ia	17,297	10,564	7,813	4,262	4,692	110.1
..th America (2)	2,729,661	2,927,525	2,700,030	2,767,355	2,844,651	102.8
..e, 7 countries prev.						
..pt'd and unchanged ..	447,100	465,573	533,548	343,509	276,142	80.4
..i, revised	26,548	24,210	17,186	26,104	23,877	91.5
..ary, revised	60,813	87,971	76,548	68,347	43,324	63.4
..al Europe (9)	534,461	581,754	627,282	437,960	343,343	78.4
..: European total ex.						
..ussia	581,000	626,000	665,000	479,000		
..:a (3)	4,326	4,362	4,719	5,127	6,995	136.4
..ion Republic,revised	(900)	433	472	512	433	84.6
..ite	(115)	(118)	276	354	236	66.7
..uria, revised	(27,000)	43,206	72,144	72,832	71,238	97.8
..al Asia (3)	(28,015)	43,757	72,892	73,698	71,907	97.6
..al N. Hemis. (17) ..	3,296,463	3,557,398	3,406,075	3,284,140	3,266,896	99.5
..: N. Hemis. total						
..t. Russia	3,681,000	3,907,000	3,777,000	3,647,000		
..: world total ex.						
..ussia	4,126,000	4,530,000	4,445,000	4,311,000		

..igures in parenthesis indicate the number of countries included.

RICE: Second and final estimates of acreage in India,
                       1922 to 1928

Year	Second estimate	Final estimate
	1,000 acres	1,000 acres
..922	78,455	82,401
..923	75,455	78,932
..924	77,763	81,328
..925	78,149	82,378
..926	77,128	79,718
..927	74,657	77,790
..928	79,256	

FEED GRAINS: Movement from principal exporting countries

Item	Net exports for year		Shipments 1928, week ended a/			Net movement as far as reported		
	1926-27	1927-28	Dec. 1	Dec. 8	Dec. 15	July 1 to and incl.	1927-28	1928-
BARLEY, EXPORTS:	1,000	1,000	1,000	1,000	1,000		1,000	1,00
Year beginning July 1	bushels	bushels	bushels	bushels	bushels		bushels	bushe
United States ..	17,044	36,580	114	804	588	Dec.15	28,107	41,6
Canada	42,533	25,131				Nov.30	12,016	21,6
Argentina	14,217	b/11,192	b/ 25			Dec. 1	b/ 1,367	b/ 1
Danubian countries b/	26,508	27,242	700			Dec. 1	20,967	14,4
Total	100,302	100,145					62,457	77,8
OATS, EXPORTS:								
Year beginning July 1								
United States .	15,041	9,823	111	230	349	Dec.15	5,359	9,6
Canada	13,396	10,180				Nov.30	2,892	10,9
Argentina	40,008	b/ 29,455	b/ 68			Dec. 1	b/8,882	b/ 7
Danubian countries b/	858	878	0			Dec. 1	556	
Total	69,303	50,336					17,689	21,

	Net exports for year		Weekly a/ shipments, 1928, week ended				Total for sea including lat week shown	
	1926-27	1927-28	Nov. 24	Dec. 1	Dec. 8	Dec. 15	1927-28	192
CORN, EXPORTS:	1,000	1,000	1,000	1,000	1,000	1,000	1,000	1,
Year beginning November 1	bushels	bushels	bushels	bushels	bushels	bushels	bushels	bus
United States .	17,145	20,556	350	973	1,699	1,443	1,445	5,
Danubian countries b/	36,557	15,266	0	0			2,057	
Argentina	322,876	c271,970	b/3,776	b/3,707	b/5,751	b/4,249	38,464	b/28,
Union of South Africa	8,562	d/24,257	d/ 600	d/ 600			d/ 2,571	d/ 3,
IMPORTS:								
Year beginning November 1								
United States .	5,042	1,436						
Total exports less U. S. imports	380,098	330,613					44,537	

Compiled from official and trade sources. a/ The weeks shown in these columns nearest to the date shown. b/ Trade sources. c/ Trade sources since May. d/ Unofficial reports of exports to Europe for South and East Africa.

COTTON: Area and production in countries reporting for 1928-29,
with comparisons

Item and Country	Average 1909-19 to 1913-14	1926-27	1927-28	1928-29	Per cent 1928-29 is of 1927-28
	1,000 acres	1,000 acres	1,000 acres	1,000 acres	Per cent
AREA					
United States	34,152	47,087	40,138	45,326	112.9
Uganda	58	570	540	698	129.3
India a/	22,503	24,003	23,178	24,992	107.8
Other countries previously reported and unchanged b/	3,759	5,046	4,734	5,429	114.6
Total above countries ..	60,472	76,706	68,590	76,445	111.4
Estimated world total excluding China	62,300	80,900	73,800	–	–
	1,000 bales	1,000 bales	1,000 bales	1,000 bales	Per cent
PRODUCTION c/					
United States	13,033	17,977	12,955	14,373	110.9
Chosen	20	145	135	148	109.6
Egypt	1,453	1,586	1,252	1,490	119.0
India	3,585	4,269	4,597	5,018	109.2
Other countries previously reported and unchanged d/	1,114	1,265	1,292	1,608	124.4
Total above countries ..	19,205	25,242	20,231	22,637	111.9
Estimated world total including China	20,900	28,900	23,800	–	–

Official sources and International Institute of Agriculture except as
otherwise stated.
a/   India estimates for post-war years are December estimates.
b/   Includes Egypt, Russia, Mexico, Chosen, Bulgaria, Algeria, Syria, Anglo-
Egyptian Sudan, and Alaouite.
c/   In vales of 478 pounds net.
d/   Includes Russia, Mexico, Anglo-Egyptian Sudan, and Tanganyika.

SUGAR BEETS: Acreage and production, average 1909-1913, annual 1925-1928

Country a/	Average 1909-1913	1925	1926	1927	1928 prelim-imary	Per cent 1928 is of 1927
ACREAGE	Acres	Acres	Acres	Acres	Acres	Per cent
Canada	16,724	43,418	46,988	44,103	51,294	116.3
United States	485,495	647,000	677,000	721,000	646,000	90.0
Total N.America (2).	502,219	6 90,418	723,988	765,103	697,294	91.1
Europe, 15 count. prev rept'd & unchanged .	3,551,619	3,693,415	3,704,903	4,331,600	4,598,924	106.2
Denmark	80,310	93,105	73,636	104,721	113,172	108.1
Netherlands	144,236	163,140	152,125	170,504	161,245	94.6
Belgium	145,959	178,327	158,206	174,564	156,207	89.5
Italy	130,469	141,000	196,900	218,609	269,463	123.3
Germany	b/1,074,979	995,902	995,652	1,072,267	1,122,617	104.7
Austria	57,063	49,862	48,904	60,393	69,682	115.4
Hungary	130,620	162,835	156,417	159,447	163,914	102.8
Total Europe (22) ..	5,315,235	5,477,587	5,486,743	6,292,111	6,655,224	105.
Total above 24 count	5,817,474	6,168,005	6,210,731	7,057,214	7,352,518	104
World total c/	5,818,290	6,169,885	6,212,531	7,060,014		
PRODUCTION	Short tons	Short tons	Short tons	Short tons	Short tons	
Canada	159,600	458,200	525,000	391,000	427,000	109.2
United States	4,860,200	7,366,000	7,223,000	7,753,000	7,040,000	90.8
Total N. America (2)	5,019,800	7,824,200	7,748,000	8,144,000	7,467,000	91.7
Europe, 9 count. prev. rept'd & unchanged d/..	32,049,416	31,451,833	28,887,976	30,871,345	28,114,000	91.1
Italy	1,982,632	1,735,000	2,532,000	2,221,564	3,154,000	142.0
Austria	560,689	342,965	529,352	796,632	777,673	97.6
Hungary	1,512,717	1,683,665	1,692,400	1,604,311	1,212,761	75.6
Russia	10,635,667	7,617,900	7,042,000	10,872,000	10,465,000	96.3
Total Europe (13) ..	46,741,121	43,031,363	40,584,228	46,365,852	43,723,434	94.3
Total above 15 count	51,760,921	50,855,563	48,332,228	54,509,852	51,190,434	93 c
World total c/	61,577,898	62,752,185	58,957,734	67,195,067		

Official sources and International Institute of Agriculture.
a/   Figures in parenthesis indicate the number of countries included.
b/   One year only, 1912.
c/   Exclusive cf acreage and production in minor producing countries for which no data are available.
d/   See Foreign Crops and Markets, November 26, 1928, page 840.

FLAXSEED: Acreage in specified countries and estimated world total, average 1909-1913, annual 1921-1928 ..

	Estimated world total		United States	Canada	Argentina	India	Russia
	Excluding Russia	Including Russia					
	1,000 acres	1,000 acres	1,000 acres	1,000 acres	1,000 acres	1,000 acres	1,000 acres
erage 1909-1913.	12,705	15,870	2,490	1,035	4,113	3,825	3,165
21	9,576	11,548	1,108	533	3,892	3,011	1,972
22	10,454	12,614	1,113	565	4,317	3,382	2,160
23	12,954	15,270	2,014	630	5,391	3,724	2,316
24	16,073	19,033	3,469	1,277	6,323	3,695	2,960
25	15,245	19,143	3,078	843	6,201	3,596	3,898
26	15,072	19,239	2,907	738	6,672	3,331	4,167
27	15,206	19,557	2,906	476	7,055	3,352	4,351
28 a/	---	---	2,831	349	7,297	---	4,292

Preliminary.

- - - - - - - - - - -

Soybeans and peanuts in the United States and soybeans in Manchurai, 1909 and 1921-1928

	United States		Manchuria, soybeans
Year	Peanuts	Soybeans a/	Production
	1,000 acres	1,000 acres	1,000 short tons
1909	b/ 870	---	c/
1921	1,214	---	---
1922	1,005	314	---
1923	896	452	2,623
1924	1,187	490	3,186
1925	958	431	---
1926	843	543	3,568
1927	1,128	653	5,235
1928	1,185	---	6,138

a/ Acreage of beans gathered, does not include a larger acreage grown for grazing or purposes other than for gathering.
b/ United States Census.
c/ Source: Consular service quoting reports of the Research Bureau of the South Manchurian Railway.

GRAINS: Exports from the United States, July 1-December 15, 1927 and 1928
PORK: Exports from the United States, January 1-December 15, 1927 and 1928

	July 1-Dec. 15		1928, week ending			
Commodity	1927	1928	Nov.24	Dec. 1	Dec.8	Dec.15
GRAINS:	1,000 bushels	1,000 bushels	1,000 bushels	1,000 bushels	1,000 bushels	1,000 bushels
Wheat a/	121,162	69,804	1,584	1,291	3,757	1,675
Wheat flour b/	31,138	25,389	870	512	1,090	949
Rye	19,571	7,864	84	2	609	106
Corn	3,373	8,318	350	973	1,699	1,443
Oats	3,724	7,832	204	111	230	349
Barley a/	30,133	40,963	388	114	804	588
PORK:	Jan. 1-Dec. 15					
	1,000 pounds	1,000 pounds	1,000 pounds	1,000 pounds	1,000 pounds	1,000 pounds
Hams & shoulders,incl. Wiltshire sides	114,261	114,760	1,426	687	1,006	698
Bacon,incl.Cumberland sides	110,583	116,637	1,444	1,200	1,333	3,382
Lard	644,736	698,612	14,153	12,581	9,483	22,778
Pickled pork	27,965	29,922	365	149	269	156

Compiled from official records, Bureau of Foreign and Domestic Commerce.a/ Included this week: Pacific ports wheat 972,000 bush., flour 30,000 bbls; San Francisco barley 53,000 bush. b/ Includes milled in bond from Canadian wheat, in terms of wheat.

WHEAT, INCLUDING FLOUR: Shipments from principal exporting countries

	Net exports		Shipments week ending nearest given date,1928			Net movement from July as far as reported		
Country	1926-27	1927-28 a/	Dec. 1	Dec. 8	Dec. 15	To and incl.	1927-28	1928-29
Canada:	1,000 bush.	1,000 bush.	1,000 bush.	1,000 bush.	1,000 bush.	Date	1,000 bush.	1,000 bush.
Exports- Official ... 5 ports,Brad.	304,540	305,182				Nov.30	bc121,617	bc225,573
b/	177,370	238,730	9,718	7,259	6,733	Dec.15	115,540	170,792
Shipments- 4 markets d/b/	297,961	b/326,361	31,648	21,577	11,373	Dec.15	197,988	306,653
Pub.elev.in east b/...			7,989	2,673	--	Dec.8	81,807	134,675
United States.	205,896	190,927	1,803	4,847	2,624	Dec.15	e148,617	e 87,853
Argentina	139,790	186,000	3,804	3,365	3,407	Dec.15	33,458	54,624
Australia	96,584	72,962	1,168	1,480	1,536	Dec.15	22,076	25,236
Russia	49,202	7,000	0	0	0	Dec.15	5,392	8
Hungary	21,142	22,133	)					
Yugoslavia ...	10,216	1,000	)					
Rumania	11,388	5,000	) 0	104	64	Dec.15	3,592	1,848
Bulgaria	2,236	2,125	)					
British India.	8,660	12,264	0	0	0	Dec.15	8,224	1,064
Total	849,654	804,593	38,423	31,373	19,004		419,347	477,286

Compiled from official and trade sources. a/Prelim. b/Excluded from total.c/ Exports through Nov.less imports through Sept. d/Total shipments from Ft.William, Port Arthur,Vancouver,and Prince Rupert. e/ Exports through Dec.15 less imports through Oct.

BUTTER: Prices in London, Berlin, Copenhagen and New York, in cents per pound
(Foreign prices by weekly cable)

Market and Item	December 22, 1927	December 13, 1928	December 20, 1928
	Cents	Cents	Cents
New York, 92 score	52.00	50.50	49.50
Copenhagen, official quotation .	36.23	44.25	43.03
Berlin, la quality	38.25	44.08	46.02
London: a/			
Danish	39.97	45.19	45.84
Dutch, unsalted	40.41	46.06	46.71
New Zealand	34.54	39.97	39.97
New Zealand, unsalted	36.93	42.58	42.60
Australian	33.67	39.54	39.76
Australian, unsalted	35.20	40.19	40.41
Argentine, unsalted	33.67	38.24	36.87
Siberian	32.15	b/	39.11

Quotations converted at par of exchange. a/ Quotations of following day.
b/ No quotation.

- - - - - - - - - - -

EUROPEAN LIVESTOCK AND MEAT MARKETS
(By weekly cable)

Market and Item	Unit	Week ended Dec.21, 1927	Dec.12, 1928	Dec.19, 1928
GERMANY:				
Receipt of hogs, 14 markets ..	Number	99,225	72,870	95,991
Prices of hogs, Berlin	$ per 100 lbs.	12.61	15.94	15.83
Prices of lard, tcs.,Hamburg .	"	13.96	13.96	14.01
UNITED KINGDOM AND IRELAND:				
Hogs, certain markets,England	Number	18,688	21,364	23,347
Prices at Liverpool:				
Prime Steam Western lard a/ .	$ per 100 lbs.	13.47	13.14	13.24
American Short cut green hams	"	23.25	24.88	24.77
American green bellies	"	18.25	18.68	18.47
Danish Wiltshire sides	"	17.81	22.59	21.72

a/ Friday quotation.

- - - - - - - - - - -

Index